GET OUT ALIVE!

ESCAPE FROM A DEATH ROLL

Julie K. Lundgren

Published in the United States of America by Cherry Lake Publishing Group
Ann Arbor, Michigan
www.cherrylakepublishing.com

Reading Adviser: Beth Walker Gambro, MS, Ed., Reading Consultant, Yorkville, IL

Photo Credits:
© Lauren Suryanata/Shutterstock, cover, (crocodile), © Sergey Uryadnikov/Shutterstock cover (water buffalo), page 15 (top), page 16 (top), © fiestachka/Shutterstock (graphic on cover and throughout book); © Cassette Bleue/Shutterstock, speech bubbles throughout; © Nazarkru/Shutterstock, yellow bursts throughout; © Alexander Machulskiy/Shutterstock contents (crocodile); © Lauren Suryanata/Shutterstock page 4, page 9; © AlevtinaGorskaya/Shutterstock (top), © Eibran Atencio/Shutterstock, © Pyty/Shutterstock (map) page 5; © Elenarts/Shutterstock page 6; © udaix/Shutterstock (life cycle illustration), © Supermop/Shutterstock (baby alligators), © Rizky Ade Jonathan/Shutterstock page 7; © Danny Ye/Shutterstock page 8; © Vitamin/Shutterstock (photo of rough water), © redgreystock/Shutterstock (splash graphic), © GUDKOV ANDREY/Shutterstock (bottom) page 10; © Michal Sanca/Shutterstock (basketball player), © dwi putra stock/Shutterstock (croc in green box), © Tracey Jones Photography/Shutterstock page 11; © kung_tom/Shutterstock page 12; © imageBROKER.com/Shutterstock (top), © Peter is Shaw 1991/Shutterstock (horns on car), © Roman Chekhovskoi/Shutterstock (car – editorial use only) page 13; © Endemic India/Shutterstock page 14; © Bison photo from Shutterstock, © Peyker/Shutterstock (sword) page 15; © npSpot/Shutterstock (bottom); © JWhitwell/Shutterstock (top), © Susan Flashman/Shutterstock (bottom) page 17; © Wayne Marinovich/Shutterstock page 18, and page 23 (top); © Nilanka Sampath/Shutterstock (top), © Fluid and Framed/Shutterstock page 19; © KrongPhoto/Shutterstock (top), © Willyam Bradberry/Shutterstock page 20; © Alexander Machulskiy/Shutterstock (top), © Wayne Marinovich/Shutterstock page 21; © Roberto Dani/Shutterstock (croc), © Fernandodiass/Shutterstock (POW!) page 22; © Sazid Rezwan/Shutterstock (bottom) page 23.

Produced for Cherry Lake Publishing by bluedooreducation.com

Copyright © 2026 by Cherry Lake Publishing Group

All rights reserved. No part of this book may be reproduced or utilized in any form or by any means without written permission from the publisher.

Library of Congress Cataloging-in-Publication Data has been filed and is available at catalog.loc.gov.

Printed in the United States of America

Note from Publisher: Websites change regularly, and their future contents are outside of our control. Supervise children when conducting any recommended online searches for extended learning opportunities.

About the Author

Julie K. Lundgren grew up in northern Minnesota near Lake Superior. She delighted in picking berries, finding cool rocks, and trekking in the woods. She still does! Julie's interest in nature science led her to a degree in biology. She adores her family, her sweet cat, and Adventure Days.

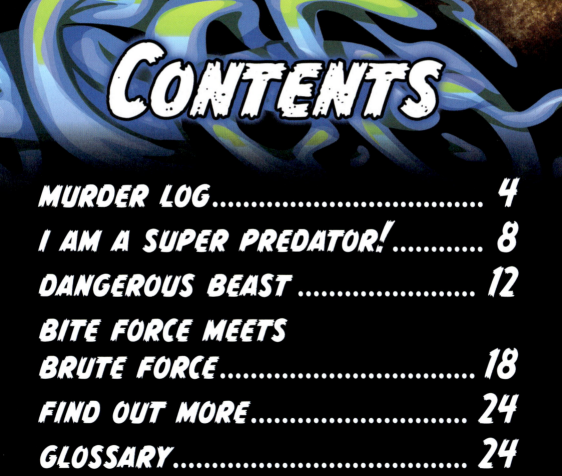

Contents

MURDER LOG 4
I AM A SUPER PREDATOR! 8
DANGEROUS BEAST 12
BITE FORCE MEETS BRUTE FORCE 18
FIND OUT MORE 24
GLOSSARY 24
INDEX 24

MURDER LOG

People in Australia call us salties.

Powerful, *nocturnal* hunters lurk in still, salty waters. With only eyes showing, the croc hides in the water. Is it a log or a floating killer?

SALTWATER CROCODILES LIVE IN MANY PLACES, FROM INDIA AND SOUTHEAST ASIA TO AUSTRALIA.

I AM A SUPER PREDATOR!

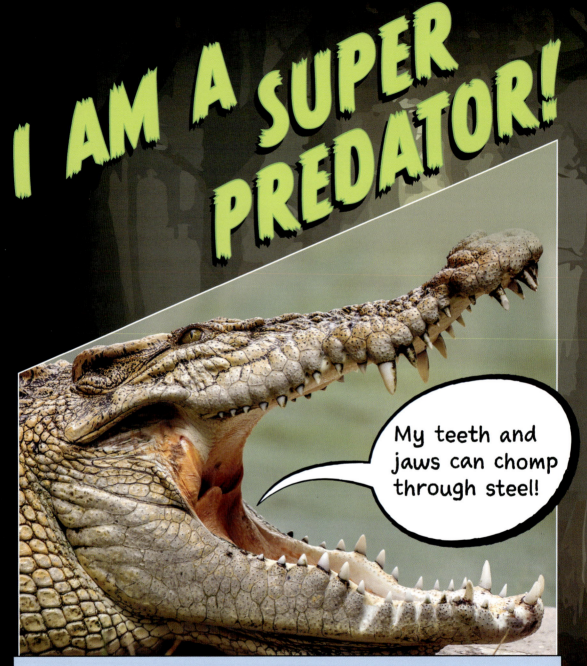

My teeth and jaws can chomp through steel!

Crocs have strong muscles and jagged teeth. They also have the strongest bite force of any land animal. That makes them top predators.

Most scary of all is the croc's death roll. It clamps its jaws on prey. Then its strong body spins underwater.

SPLASH!

DURING A DEATH ROLL, THE PREY DROWNS WHILE THE CROC SHAKES OFF ITS BODY PARTS.

SALTIES ATTACK PEOPLE, TOO.

PROBABLE NUMBER OF ATTACKS IN A YEAR:

Country	Attacks
INDONESIA	170
INDIA	107
MALAYSIA	21
AUSTRALIA	16
PAPUA NEW GUINEA	14

ALMOST HALF THE ATTACKS END IN A CROC'S LUNCH.

HOW BIG IS A SALTIE?

A 20-FOOT (6.1-METER) SALTWATER CROCODILE IS AS BIG AS A STACK OF LEBRON JAMES TRIPLETS.

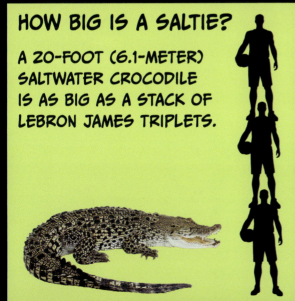

DANGEROUS BEAST

WATER BUFFALO ESCAPE THE HEAT IN SMALL HERDS. THEY DIG INTO THE MUD AND **WALLOW** IN MUDDY POOLS.

Wild water buffalo eat plants that grow in and around the water.

WATER BUFFALO HORNS SLASH AND SLICE. THEIR HORNS LOOK LIKE SHARP, CURVED **SWORDS**.

AMERICAN **BISON** ARE ALSO CALLED BUFFALO. THEY ARE STRONG AND EAT GRASS, TOO, BUT THEY ARE NOT THE SAME ANIMAL.

15

What about Australia? No wild water buffalo live there. What do crocs eat? They eat wallabies, kangaroos, snakes, and other animals that come to the water to drink.

KANGAROO

YELLOW-FOOTED ROCK-WALLABY

BITE FORCE MEETS BRUTE FORCE

The Sun's heat drives a small herd of water buffalo to the river to cool off. They look for danger. Then they wade in. Most of the herd stays close to shore.

They don't see the croc floating nearby. His eyes peek out of the water. He is on the hunt!

One buffalo moves deeper to escape pesky flies. The croc silently slips underwater. He swims toward the buffalo.

The croc didn't see that move coming! The kick buys time for the buffalo to get back to its herd. Safe!

The croc drifts off to find easier prey.

Find Out More

Books

Murray, Julie. *Saltwater Crocodile*, North Mankato, MN: Abdo Publishing, 2021

Hansen, Grace. *Water Buffalo*, North Mankato, MN: Abdo Publishing, 2021

Websites

Search these online sources with an adult:

Saltwater crocodile | kiddle
Water buffalo | Britannica

Glossary

ambush (AM-bush) a sneaky, hidden attack

bison (BIE-suhn) large, hoofed grass-eaters of North America, related to cattle

bite force (BYTE FORS) the amount of strength or energy in an animal's bite

extinct (ik-STINGKT) no longer found alive

lunges (LUN-jehz) attacks with speed

nocturnal (nok-TER-nuhl) active at night

predators (PREH-duh-terz) animals that hunt and eat other animals

swords (SORDZ) weapons with handles and sharp blades

wallabies (WAWL-uh-beez) furry, hopping Australian animals that look like small kangaroos

wallow (WAHL-oh) to wade and rest in mud or water with enjoyment

Index

death roll   10
dinosaurs   6
eye(s)   4, 19, 22
herd(s)   12, 18, 23
kick(ing)   14, 22, 23
hooves   14
horns   13, 14, 15
prey   10, 23
speed   14, 21
tail   13, 21
teeth   8
water   4, 9, 10, 12, 17, 19